Angling

The Joy of Angling in Scotland

A Selection of Classic Articles on the Best Fishing Locations in Scotland

By

Various Authors

Copyright © 2011 Read Books Ltd.
This book is copyright and may not be
reproduced or copied in any way without
the express permission of the publisher in writing

British Library Cataloguing-in-Publication Data
A catalogue record for this book is available from
the British Library

A Short History of Fishing

Fishing, in its broadest sense – is the activity of catching fish. It is an ancient practice dating back at least 40,000 years. Since the sixteenth century fishing vessels have been able to cross oceans in pursuit of fish and since the nineteenth century it has been possible to use larger vessels and in some cases process the fish on board. Techniques for catching fish include varied methods such as hand gathering, spearing, netting, angling and trapping.

Isotopic analysis of the skeletal remains of **Tianyuan man**, a 40,000 year old modern human from eastern Asia, has shown that he regularly consumed freshwater fish. As well as this, archaeological features such as shell middens, discarded fish-bones and cave paintings show that sea foods were important for early man's survival and were consumed in significant quantities. The first civilisation to practice organised fishing was the Egyptians however, as the River Nile was so full of fish. The **Egyptians** invented various implements and methods for fishing and these are clearly illustrated in tomb scenes, drawings and papyrus documents. Simple **reed boats** served for fishing. Woven nets, weir baskets made from willow branches, harpoons and hook and line (the hooks having a length of between eight millimetres and eighteen centimetres) were all being used. By the twelfth dynasty, metal hooks with barbs were also utilised.

Despite the Egyptian's strong history of fishing, later Greek cultures rarely depicted the trade, due to its perceived low social status. There is a wine cup however, dating from c.500 BC, that shows a boy crouched on a rock with a fishing-rod in his right hand and a basket in his left. In the water below there is a rounded object of the same material with an opening on the top. This has been identified as a fish-cage used for keeping live fish, or as a fish-trap. One of the other major Grecian sources on fishing is Oppian of Corycus, who wrote a major treatise on sea fishing, the *Halieulica* or *Halieutika*, composed between 177 and 180. This is the earliest such work to have survived intact to the modern day. Oppian describes various means of fishing including the use of nets cast from boats, scoop nets held open by a hoop, spears and tridents, and various traps 'which work while their masters sleep.' Oppian's description of fishing with a 'motionless' net is also very interesting:

> *The fishers set up very light nets of buoyant flax and wheel in a circle round about while they violently strike the surface of the sea with their oars and make a din with sweeping blow of poles. At the*

flashing of the swift oars and the noise the fish bound in terror and rush into the bosom of the net which stands at rest, thinking it to be a shelter: foolish fishes which, frightened by a noise, enter the gates of doom. Then the fishers on either side hasten with the ropes to draw the net ashore...

The earliest English essay on recreational fishing was published in 1496, shortly after the invention of the printing press! Unusually for the time, its author was a woman; Dame Juliana Berners, the prioress of the Benedictine Sopwell Nunnery (Hertforshire). The essay was titled *Treatyse of Fysshynge with an Angle* and was published in a larger book, forming part of a treatise on hawking, hunting and heraldry. These were major interests of the nobility, and the publisher, Wynkyn der Worde was concerned that the book should be kept from those who were not gentlemen, since their immoderation in angling might 'utterly destroye it.' The roots of recreational fishing itself go much further back however, and the earliest evidence of the fishing reel comes from a fourth century AD work entitled *Lives of Famous Mortals*.

Many credit the first recorded use of an artificial fly (fly fishing) to an even earlier source - to the Roman Claudius Aelianus near the end of the second century.

He described the practice of Macedonian anglers on the Astraeus River, '...they have planned a snare for the fish, and get the better of them by their fisherman's craft. ... They fasten red wool round a hook, and fit on to the wool two feathers which grow under a cock's wattles, and which in colour are like wax.' Recreational fishing for sport or leisure only really took off during the sixteenth and seventeenth centuries though, and coincides with the publication of Izaak Walton's *The Compleat Angler* in 1653. This is seen as the definitive work that champions the position of the angler who loves fishing for the sake of fishing itself. More than 300 editions have since been published, demonstrating its unstoppable popularity.

Big-game fishing only started as a sport after the invention of the motorised boat. In 1898, Dr. Charles Frederick Holder, a marine biologist and early conservationist, virtually invented this sport and went on to publish many articles and books on the subject. His works were especially noted for their combination of accurate scientific detail with exciting narratives. Big-game fishing is also a recreational pastime, though requires a largely purpose built boat for the hunting of large fish such as the billfish (swordfish, marlin and sailfish), larger tunas (bluefin, yellowfin and bigeye), and sharks (mako, great white, tiger and hammerhead). Such developments have only really gained prominence in the twentieth century. The motorised boat has also meant that commercial fishing, as well as fish farming has emerged on a massive scale. Large trawling ships are common and one of the strongest markets in the world is the cod trade which fishes roughly 23,000 tons from the Northwest Atlantic, 475,000 tons from the Northeast Atlantic and 260,000 tons from the Pacific.

These truly staggering amounts show just how much fishing has changed; from its early hunter-gatherer beginnings, to a small and specialised trade in Egyptian and Grecian societies, to a gentleman's pastime in fifteenth century England right up to the present day. We hope that the reader enjoys this book, and is inspired by fishing's long and intriguing past to find out more about this truly fascinating subject. Enjoy.

Contents

Expectation and Realisation. Craigvinean………………..…..*page* 1

Scotland for Pike. Alexandra…………………....………..…...*page* 3

North-East for Spring Salmon. Alexandra………………..…*page* 6

Brown Trout in Scotland. H. E. Crocker……………………....*page* 10

Fishing the Strathspey. A. A. Water……………………..…….*page* 14

The Loch of the Showers. Salfario……………………....…..…*page* 17

Casting at Falkirk. Anon…………………....………..………..*page* 20

Salmon Poaching in Southern Scotland. J. F. Hampton…..….*page* 22

Frustrated by Drought. W. A. Adamson………………………...*page* 25

Tracing the Kenmure Skull. Michael Logan…………………..….*page* 27

The Hydro-Electric Controversy. W. A. Adamson…………..….*page* 32

Memories of International Day in Loch Leven. Zulu………...*page* 34

Sea-Fishing in Ross-Shire. Wanderer……………………........*page* 41

Scottish Lowland Fishing. Alexandra……………………........*page* 45

Have You Fished the Ythan. Maurice Hartley………………..*page* 48

A Scots Angling Holiday. Pat Castle……………………......…*page* 51

EXPECTATION AND REALIZATION

(*With photographs taken by the author from the train*)

by Craigvinean

AS the north-bound train steamed out of Perth, my retriever pup, Sam, and I settled down for our long journey, with due thankfulness for an empty carriage.

Various places in Scotland lay claim to the title "Gateway to the Highlands" but for hundreds of expectant anglers, Perth must be that welcome landmark, for from there onwards scarcely a mile of the train journey is unaccompanied by one river or another, and the weather forecasts and angling reports which have been studied so eagerly for days past can be gauged against the visible condition of the waters as they come into sight. A mile or so out of Perth the Tay is seen, rolling in dark majesty, showing no obvious signs of the recent dry spell, and one has a fleeting glimpse of a boat harling the pool below Scone Palace. Onwards by Tummel and Garry the railway climbs steadily to the summit of the Grampians where streaks of snow in the corries promise some replenishment of the headwaters of the eastward flowing rivers. But when Spey comes into view at Newtonmore, hope sinks sharply for the river shows but rippling shallows sparkling in the afternoon sun. As the train flies swiftly down Speyside, clouds of smoke drift over the nearer hills, betokening the activities of keepers and shepherds, heather burning while the dry spell lasts, and the rocky beds of the little burns cry aloud of days and weeks of drought. Findhorn is but a trickle of clearest crystal in a stony strath and by the time Inverness is reached the eager expectations of weeks past had shrunk to dogged hope,

Smoke clouds drift over the hills

bolstered by the knowledge that the river of our destination numbered in its pools two which were partially tidal and whose depths could be expected to hold fish at any height of water. Northward again we took our way, and Beauly and Connon raised hope from the slough of despond, for they seemed to show signs of a more purposeful flow and lacked the pellucid clearness of the Grampian watershed, then the evening sun sank behind a bank of cloud which might well be the forerunner of rain on the morrow.

By ten o'clock next morning we were at the riverside, Sam and I, he, revelling in the freedom of the gorse-clad banks and myriad rabbit burrows, and I, rejoicing in the swing of my favourite greenheart and the swish of the tapered line. The morning was cold with a strong east wind blowing in from the sea bearing with it the damp saltiness of an east-coast haar. It was by no means ideal or pleasant fishing weather.

On commencing a day's fishing it is my invariable custom to count the first twenty casts, for surely each day must begin with hope, and only the rubbing of continued failure can dull the edge of expectation. The first twenty casts pay tribute to the god of hope; and so it proved on that grey and misty morn, for as the nineteenth cast swung from the jabble of the stream into the calm of the pool beyond, the rod bent and the reel spoke loud and clear. What a mixture of joy and fear went to the playing of that fish, and it was not till a lovely little eight-pounder lay still on the turf that I breathed freely once more.

And the morning and the evening were the first day, and the second, and the third also.

Three whole days; days of hard labour and ever-present hope, for the river was teeming with fish, fish that rolled and splashed, gleaming in silvery beauty, deceitful as is the lust of gain.

As we boarded the train that bore us south, Sam and I were content.

The river was teeming with fish

SCOTLAND FOR PIKE
by Alexandra

In Scotland, where pike are ignored and fishing for them is generally free, there is fine sport awaiting those who will travel a little further to get it.

SOUTHERNERS are not averse, I understand, to paying good money for first-class pike fishing and for them a country where the natives seldom think of pike fishing is a matter worthy of consideration. It is, therefore, somewhat strange that so few fishermen south of the border have any idea that in Scotland they can fish almost any water for coarse fish; and that most of the owners of rivers and lochs welcome anglers who will thin out the pike and perch for them.

Let me then name some of the places where heavy pike and perch abound, which are at the same time beautiful spots in which to spend a holiday. This last requirement is important, for many members of angler's families do not fish and would have cause to complain bitterly if dumped at some far-off northern fishing inn, with nothing to do but watch the mist on the mountains.

Across the Border north of Carlisle there is the small town of Lochmaben, between Lockerbie, on the main Glasgow road, and Dumfries. This small township is set amidst four lochans which offer grand pike fishing; and the river Annan, a fine water not only for salmon, sea-trout, herling and brown trout, but for pike and chub also, is only a mile or two distant.

The Lochar, a sluggish stream which winds its way through the low-lying moss between Lochmaben and Dum-

Loch Ken in Kirkcudbrightshire has always been famed for its pike

fries, yields good pike also, as does the Nith, which flows through Dumfries. Loch Ken, a long narrow enlargement of the waters of Ken and Dee between New Galloway and Castle Douglas, is also good pike water and the charge for fishing is nominal. There are, besides, several little lochs in Dumfriesshire and Kirkcudbrightshire, which are disdained by trout fishermen, but which nevertheless hold plenty of pike and perch, and local advice as to the best of these is readily available.

Loch Lomond, which is, of course, a fine salmon and sea-trout water, holds many large pike. The trout and coarse fishing is free here, but the salmon and sea trout fishing costs 12s. 6d. per day; and boats can be hired from Balloch, a bright little place at the foot of the loch, where there are, moreover, plenty of hotels. This is an ideal spot for non-fishing members of the family. A comfortable steamer zigzags between the east and west shores daily and calls at all piers where a landing can be made and the boat rejoined when it returns later in the day.

Loch Achray, a lovely water set in perfect surroundings, overshadowed by the high peaks of Ben A'an and Ben Venue in the Trossachs, offers good sport to pike fishers and there are hotels on the waterside with boats available.

At the western end of Loch Vennachar which is only a few miles away, there is good pike fishing, and close at hand to the south-west is the Lake of Menteith, which is full of big pike and perch. This delightfully pretty lake is quite unspoiled, and its shores are as quiet and peaceful as they were a century ago.

Further north lies Loch Awe, famous for its trout fishing, but at the eastern end, near Dalmally, big pike are caught in the weedy shallows near the rivers of Kilchurn Castle, and not a few pike

4

fishermen from the south think this is Scotland's best.

If the main north road through Perth is taken, there is a chain of charmingly situated reedy lochs on the road between Dunkeld and Blairgowrie, where the pike and perch fishing is excellent, as troops stationed there during the war soon discovered; and permission to fish is easily obtained.

Loch Tummel, west of Pitlochry, is famed for its big pike, and its recent enlargement due to the Hydro Electric Scheme does not appear to have affected the fishing adversely. Much further north, on the main road, where it has crossed the Drumochter Pass and Strathspey, one reaches Loch Insh, a widening of the river Spey near Kingussie. There are some good pike here; and a little farther on the way to Inverness we come to Loch Alvie, a pretty little water near Aviemore, which also contains substantial pike.

These are but a few of the good places for pike fishing in Scotland, there are many more. Almost anywhere one can find hill lochs holding pike, but pointed questioning and a clear statement of what your require is necessary if you are to find them, because no one ever thinks that a visitor wants to fish for pike. Hotel proprietors, boatmen, gillies and tackle dealers are all so used to visitors being interested only in salmon, sea-trout and brown trout that they never think of mentioning the grand but neglected pike-fishing which may be close at hand. Should a likely loch be spotted when touring and you ask if there are any fish in it, the reply may well be: "No, nothing but pike and perch." But with southern waters becoming more crowded and less fruitful each year, as more and more anglers fish them, this grand Scottish coarse fishing is getting better known; and a tour planned to include a few nights in some of the centres described would make a wonderful winter (or summer) holiday for any fisherman keen to explore new waters and to battle with big fish. These venues are well worth investigation by any keen pike fisherman.

Loch Alvie, a beauty spot near Aviemore on the Great North Road, holds large pike

NORTH-EAST FOR SPRING SALMON by Alexandra

THE fine early rivers in Scotland's far north-eastern corner are too remote to attract the newcomer to salmon-fishing unless strong recommendation by a friend has emphasized their claims. The journey from the south as far as Inverness is considered by many to be a serious undertaking, especially in early spring; and the north-eastern rivers are a long way past this destination.

Whether by road or rail it is a long and weary journey, for distances are great even as the seagull flies, and the writhings of the railway to avoid steep hills and of the road to get round the great firths make the added mileage substantial. But this is the region of the spring rivers, with salmon-fishing starting on January 11, and a good run of fish running up long before the opening day.

A strange coast, this, to those who make their first visit. When Brora is reached, the wayfarer is still in the surroundings of the Moray Firth, with a flat shore belt and grand sandy beaches; but soon the great cliffs start to rear their grim faces from the sea, and on the rising shore-line the trees become sparse. The short river Brora is a good little water for salmon, and the town is an attractive centre, with good hotels and a fine golf course.

Helmsdale lies in a cleft in the cliffs, clustered round the northern end of the river bridge. Fine salmon-fishing here for those who can afford it, and a very pleasant little place for a spring holiday. Away up in the hills is Scotland's main goldfield, where the precious metal has been mined and washed from time immemorial. Plenty of gold is still there, but so distributed that its recovery is not an economic proposition even at today's prices.

North of Helmsdale the road forsakes the shore and rises on to the moorland, skirting the Ord of Caithness and crossing the county boundary, and now the peaks of Morven and Scaraben loom up to the west as the way drops down Berriedale

The river Brora, in Sutherland, on its short course to the sea

Hill to the surprisingly wooded valley of the Langwell Water. Down on shore level the scene is as unlike the typical Caithness landscape as can be imagined, for trees choke the sides of the river, and in this sheltered nook everything grows quickly. The antler-covered walls of the old smithy must be one of the most photographed sights in the county, the cars of the camera-wielders causing much obstruction to other vehicles whose drivers are trying to get up speed to surmount the northern side of the famous hill.

Next comes Dunbeath, another little valley village, not quite so striking as Berriedale but an attractive place for a quiet holiday.

At the cluster of buildings which compose Latheron, Latheronwheel and Forse, an inland road strikes across the moors for Thurso, a long, straight and narrow route across twenty-four miles of what has been described as nothing. The flat, brown Caithness plain stretches to the horizon on all sides, featureless and forbidding, and, save for the few houses at Mybster and Georgemas Junction, where the railway makes a surprising appearance, there is little to be seen but the stone-flag fences which are such an unusual feature of Caithness. Fine, strong fences they make, these great flagstones set on edge; and the raw material is at hand in quantity, the roadside quarries showing its accessibility. Barn-roofs are also made of the basic material, neatly joined with light coloured mortar. Much thatch is also to be seen, especially on the older and mostly abandoned crofts, though some good examples of neat, modern thatching are also found.

Eventually the wayfarer sees the narrow ribbon of the famous Thurso river winding its sinuous course through the moor to the left; and Halkirk village comes into view, a favourite centre for the salmon-fishing. The river is excellent and the fishing is very popular in the spring. It costs from £12 10s. to £30 per week, according to the month, but this is one of the best spring rivers in Scotland, with an enviable record of fish killed. April is generally the best month, with May next and then March and June.

Anglers stay in the hotel at Halkirk or in the Thurso hotels, which are conveniently near the best stretches. This large town of the northern coast is a bright little place, set in the great double bay between the formidable Dunnet Head and Holburn Head. At Scrabster, a mile round the bay, the Orkney steamer plies its busy trade to the islands. Sir John Square is the centre of the modern Thurso, where the streets are broad and rectangular in plan. In the old fisherman's quarter, down by the inner harbour, the streets are neither broad nor follow any known geometrical plan, but the huddle of quaint little whitewashed houses is most attractive, with forestairs, archways, crooked gables and the remains of Old St. Peter's Church with its beautiful window tracery still intact.

In the summer evenings fishermen wade in the narrow harbour stream, "bobbing" for sea trout, their floats riding past the hulls of vessels moored to the walls. Salmon netsmen work at the river mouth, and the seine-net boats berth along the north wall. From May to July the nights are luminous in this high latitude, and darkness is only comparative, so grand sport can be had when the sea-trout are in the estuary.

Wick, reached from Thurso across the flat country where Loch Watten lies in a shallow depression, is the biggest town north of Inverness, a

Helmsdale, Sutherland, on the river Brora. There is fine salmon-fishing here for those who can afford it

busy herring port with the clean, scrubbed appearance of the east coast grey buildings.

The Wick river is cheap to fish on the Wick Angling Club water, the charge being 5s. per day or £1 per season; salmon and sea-trout are killed, but this is sometimes a dour little river, and the stranger must work hard for his fish.

Loch Watten is a famous trout loch and is fished from Thurso, Wick and other smaller places in the neighbourhood. The average is over the pound and the water is a favourite with all anglers who know it. Like a very few other lochs, an easterly *haar* or mist is when many of the local anglers hurry to fish it.

A holiday in this north-eastern corner is an experience any angler will remember with pleasure, for here at least there is room to fish and plenty to catch. Overcrowded southern waters seem far away when fishing in the unspoiled Caithness countryside. If the distances are great the reward is substantial, in pleasant memories as well as weight of catch.

THE SHARK SEASON

Over 400 sharks were landed by anglers at Looe, Cornwall, headquarters of the Shark Angling Club of Great Britain, during the 1954 season. The qualifying fish-weight for membership has been increased from 60 lb. to 75 lb. In the coming season it is expected that four more shark-boats will be in operation, making a total of about fourteen.

ANGLER'S PARADISE

Lake of the Woods, North American angling paradise, consists of 2,000 square miles of water, has 60,000 miles of shore line, between 14,000 and 16,000 islands and contains muskellunge, lake trout, northern pike, walleyes, small-mouth black bass and many other species.

BROWN TROUT IN SCOTLAND
by H. E. Crocker

SOME years ago I spent my holidays fishing in Caithness, where I stayed with my old friend Maj. Douglas at Aberdeen. We made several expeditions to the neighbouring lochs and burns where we had good sport. Douglas was a dry-fly man, while I followed the "chuck-and-chance-it" method of the wet fly.

At that time of the year, April and May, the fish were feeding freely, and, although they did not as a rule run to any great size, a quarter to three-quarter pound being about the average, they gave good sport and fought gamely before they were landed. I was using a rod I had made myself from a broken lancewood shaft of my father's dog-cart, about seven feet long, which was quite long enough for the burns. For flies I put up Blue Duns, March Browns, Coch-y-Bonddus, Greenwell's Glory and some locally tied flies which Douglas gave me and swore they were deadly in the burns. He was right—they were.

The first day we motored some distance to a burn that ran down from a loch through open country. Clumps of rushes that grew partly in the water gave good cover for the fish, but the banks, covered with coarse grass, afforded very little cover from view for us and we had to crawl on hands and knees to avoid

A narrow burn in Aberdeenshire where the author had good sport with trout

being seen. We had, too, to be careful of our shadow falling on the water. We surveyed the burn with our glasses and spotted several fish rising close under the banks where smaller streams fell into the burn.

Douglas took the opposite bank and we worked upstream towards the loch. I put up two flies only, a March Brown and a Coch-y-Bonddu to start with and cast close in by the bank, letting them drift down to the fish. For some time I failed to get a rise so I changed to a Greenwell's Glory and a local fly on the tail. My luck improved and I rose a fish close to a clump of rushes where the cast got entangled in the roots. Luckily the fish then made for open water and I was able to get the net under him. A nice fish, just under half a pound.

Farther on upstream I spotted fish feeding on flies and other insects brought down by small streams which fell into the burn. Here I varied my method and, instead of casting into the burn itself, I cast into the small stream and let it carry the flies down into the burn. Immediately I had a rise. A fish snapped at the local fly but missed it. He rose again at the next cast and this time I had him. He dashed up and down the burn, leaping high in the air and I feared for my light tackle. It held, however, and gradually he grew weaker and I was able to land him. A nice fish in good condition, between half and three-quarter pound.

We stopped for lunch, as there was not much moving, and compared baskets. We each had some good fish and had had good sport. I then wandered off taking photographs of the burn and the surrounding country, which was generally flat. We took several fish in the evening rise when the fish were snapping at clouds of small black and brown flies which just skimmed the surface of the water. They evidently preferred the natural to our own, so we packed up and made for home and supper.

The next day we made directly to the loch which was fed by a burn running in by a clump of weeds and rushes. The water ran deep under the banks and here several fish were rising as we approached, feeding on the insects brought down from upstream by the burn. They were also rising further out by the weeds. I tried Blue Duns and a Coch-y-bonddu which soon rose a fish, but I lost him through carelessness in the weeds. I changed to a local fly for a dropper which rose another fish which gave me good sport before he landed in the net. After some little time I rose a fish on the local fly which raced up and down the loch till he tired and came to the net. Several fish rose short and failed to take hold. There seemed very little doing so we stopped for lunch. That evening I waded out to where the loch shallowed and cast back under the banks where the water ran deep on either side. I soon rose a fish and played him up and down the loch for some time before I landed him. There was nothing much doing here, so I tried at the head of the loch where the feeder burn ran in close to the tall rushes. I cast out into the burn, and my flies drifted down into the loch with the natural flies. After a few casts in this manner I rose a good fish which put up a tremendous fight, tearing down into the deep water of the loch where he leaped in the air and broke the cast, getting away with my flies. I put on a March Brown and another local fly and tried again. It seemed a likely place for the fish as there was plenty of water coming down. Soon afterwards the evening rise stopped so we packed up, well pleased with our sport. The fish we caught were

A pool, fringed with rushes, where the big fish lurk

small, about three to the pound, but they were in perfect condition and fought fiercely.

The following day we fished the burns near the road below the city of Aberdeen, where they ran from a loch just under a low range of hills in the distance. I only used the tail fly, and had out little more than the cast which I found quite long enough for these narrow burns. The fish were feeding here, but at first would not look at my flies, which I changed from time to time. I then tried casting the fly on to the edge of the bank and gave it a slight twitch, thus causing it to drop into the water like a natural fly. This scored success and I hooked a good fish of just over half a pound. Some distance upstream the burn widened out into a small pool bordered on one side with rushes and weeds. After some time, trying different flies, I at length got into a good fish. Treading too near the edge of the rotten bank I fell into the water above my waist. I held the fish, however, and after a great fight brought him to the net. He was just under a pound and in splendid condition. The water was discoloured by the peat through which it ran, but we could see traces of fish rising apparently at a dark brown insect skimming closely over the surface, rather like a March Brown but somewhat darker in hue. I tried several flies before a fish would look at them but at last I rose several. I lost the first fish which rose short, and then caught a few small fish of about half a pound, which gave me a good fight with my light tackle.

That evening we worked upstream to where several smaller burns splashed into the main burn, bringing down all sorts of food on which the fish were feeding greedily. At this point I cast into one of the smaller burns and let it carry my fly—I only had on a tail fly for this cast— with the other insects. I soon had a rise, and landed a fish of about half a pound or so. Then another, slightly heavier, both on a Coch-y-Bonddu. Nothing after this for some time till a much larger fish rose to have a look at the local fly I had put on in place of the Coch-y-Bonddu. He turned away without taking it until at the third cast he finally decided that it suited his taste, and he made a grab at it. Away he went at a great rate down the burn, reeling out the line as he went. Nothing I could do would induce him to break cover from under the bank where he sulked and with my light tackle I dared not put too great a strain on the line. At length, however, he came out and I just managed to get the net under him. He was a beauty, of just under a pound and well worth the fight I had had with him.

And so ended one of the best fishing holidays I have ever had, thanks to my friend Maj. Douglas. May his lines be tight.

FELLOW FISHERS

"On reaching the river at a safe distance down, he [the water-colley, or dipper] skimmed along the surface like a kingfisher. They find abundance of insect life among the stones at the falls and everywhere in shallow water. Some accuse them of taking the ova of trout and they are shot at trout nurseries; but it is doubtful if they are really guilty, nor can they do any appreciable injury in an open stream, not being in sufficient numbers. It is the birds and other creatures peculiar to the water that render fly-fishing so pleasant; were they all destroyed, and nothing left but the mere fish, one might as well stand and fish in a stone cattle trough. I hope all true lovers of sport will assist in preserving rather than in killing them."

RICHARD JEFFERIES,
The Life of the Fields.

FISHING THE STRATHSPEY A.A. WATER by Alexandra

AS it is possibly the best bargain in salmon fishing in Scotland, the stretch of the Spey controlled by the Strathspey Angling Association is becoming very popular with visitors. It is also the venue for the courses in angling run by the Scottish Council for Physical Recreation, and many readers may be planning a visit to Speyside in the spring.

The Association's water has about thirteen miles of bank, and the novice or the stranger may well be almost embarrassed by the choice of pools, of which there are thirty-four. An excellent map of the water is given to all anglers who fish this stretch, showing the position of the pools and giving their names and numbers. It may, however, be helpful to suggest some of the most productive parts of the river, thus giving knowledge which is often gained only after long experience and sometimes too late to be of service.

The "top" of the water is at the mouth of the Nethy on the right bank and a short distance up the Dulnain on the left bank. The pools where each of these tributaries enter the river are quite good, but from them, down to where the Auchernack Burn comes in on the right bank, the possibilities are not of the best.

The Auchernack stretch is a great favourite and has many good holding pools, No. 8 (Auchernack Burn), No. 9 (Little Stream), No. 10 (Upper Bend) and No. 11 (Lower Bend) being very popular, with always a good chance of a fish. Below these four there are two small islands and the tail of these is a good place, especially for sea-trout in the summer.

Further down the river is the Inverallan stretch, consisting of pools Nos. 14, 15, 16 and 17, all good salmon-water where many fish are killed. This part has the advantage for the lazy that a car can be parked on the roadway close to each pool, whereas on many stretches of the river a good walk is necessary between vehicle and water.

Below there is the big Finnock Pool, No. 18, where good sport is had from July onwards. Two more pools and then comes the New Bridge, and between this and the Old Bridge on the lower half of the stretch, is excellent water for sea-trout, pools Nos. 23 to 27, which lie close together. Fishing from the left bank is best, if deep wading is not desired, as from the right bank the angler has to get out almost to mid-stream when the river is fairly low, the current setting towards the left bank.

Below the Old Bridge is the water which is fished by the Association only on Thursdays, Fridays and Saturdays, and a good stretch it is. The big pool, No. 29, known as the Lurg, below the bridge, is very popular, with good salmon-lies near the right hand bank, fished most easily by wading from the opposite side, as the bank is steep and tree-clad. There are also two good pools at the bottom of this "half-week" stretch, and they are directly accessible.

In most conditions anglers will find that a very early morning start gives good results, and those who fish from dawn until breakfast usually do better than the lie-a-beds. If this does not sound like holiday angling, it is, however, the best way to get fish.

For sea-trout a late evening start is best, as is usual on most rivers: and if

Fishing the Bridge Pool, below the old bridge at Grantown-on-Spey. The Strathspey Angling Association's water has about thirteen miles of bank on Speyside

A favourite stretch of the Spey near Grantown

the fishing times of the local anglers are noted, the visitor will save much time and effort and probably do better than by frantic casting all through the day.

Most strangers will be impressed by the excellent manner in which the banks are maintained. It is a pleasure to fish the Spey and an education to any association committee to see how a stretch should be kept. Well made, easily crossed stiles are found on all fences, casting-crags are plentiful whenever they are required; good, clean, undamaged huts are provided on both banks, and each pool is clearly marked with pegs on both sides giving its number.

Undergrowth on the banks is cut away as it should be, and seats are provided at many pools. At the price of £1 per week for salmon or 10s. per week for trout, it is hard to find better value than that offered by the Strathspey Association water. And, unusual in a good salmon and sea-trout river, the brown trout fishing is good and gives plenty of sport to those who prefer to fish for trout. Fly, spinning or bait is permitted, but the local fishermen mostly stick to fly and do very well with it, leaving bait-fishing for the times when the river is in flood. But Spey does not flood easily, and the stranger may well be surprised when, after a night of heavy rain, he rushes hopefully down in the morning with a can of worms, to find that the indicator shows a rise of only one inch. It takes heavy rain of fairly long duration on the hills near the source to send Spey down in a flood, and then, in sea-trout time, the visitor will have some really good sport, with a big single hook fished on the bottom.

WHERE THE ENTOMOLOGIST SCORES

"From the purely sporting point of view the angler with a knowledge of entomology possesses a great advantage, and is able readily to select a suitable fly, whereas, one without this knowledge is liable to fall into mistakes which appear grotesque to the initiated." Leonard West in his introduction to *The Natural Trout Fly and its Imitation.*

THE LOCH OF THE SHOWERS
by Salfario

"A small lake famed among anglers for the quality of its trout. I allude to ... the Loch of the Showers."

WHEN I first read this paragraph in *The Anglers' Companion,* by Thomas Tod Stoddart (1853), I merely made a mental note that here was yet one more loch in Scotland which I should never have the opportunity to fish. That was many years ago. But how the name appealed and intrigued! What were those trout like in colour, shape and gameness!

At that time I lived in London; my holidays were few and far between; moreover, they had to be spent where angling could be secured without either the trouble and expense of leasing water or depending on the generosity of some obliging tenant. Familiar streams were all I could aspire to; adventuring in strange waters was beyond me then.

I know now that The Loch of the Showers is a very private fishing. My only excuse for telling how, eventually, I came to visit The Loch of the Showers is because my experiences were, I think a little out of the ordinary.

After the passing of many years, I came to live in Scotland and, moreover, my home for two years, was within a few miles of this very loch!

One of my first thoughts was that I should fish the Loch of the Showers. But, it was by no means as easy as that. I learned from the keeper ere long that permits, even for a single day, were never issued.

Apparently this particular loch was on the march between two estates and both had the right to fish it; it was believed, however, that the right to fish was limited to the tenants, their families and relatives, and guests residing under their roofs! Later events proved that something like this was, in fact, the case.

During my second year in this district I was asked several times to shoot with the tenant, and good shooting it was. I missed no chance of telling him how much mightier I was with the rod than the gun. No matter how much I talked fishing, and he was by no means averse to talking on this subject, no reference was ever made to the Loch of the Showers!

My all too brief residence in that delightful place came to an end; though I had seen the loch several times I had cast no fly upon it.

I moved farther north and, as would happen in this strange world, the very next season a non-angling friend, wrote and said he had been invited to fish "the loch". His invitation included a second rod; would I care to join him?

There was no hesitation about my acceptance. The date fixed was in mid-July, without option.

I arrived the day before that fixed for our fishing, and a close, warm, windless day it was, until the evening. Then came a heavy thunderstorm; after which the temperature dropped and a strong wind blew from the east. And, of course, it rained in torrents.

At intervals, during the night, I could hear that rain dashing against my window, and my hopes for the morrow fell.

A car was to call at 9 a.m. to take us

The Loch of the Showers

to the keeper's house. From there we had a three miles walk over the moor.

At eight o'clock on that long anticipated morning my hostess knocked at my door and suggested that the car should be cancelled as "it's no a fit day for ye tae be oot ava let alain gannin tae that loch." She had no sooner said this than my host called from downstairs that he was *not* going to cancel the car, and at least we should go up and see the keeper.

In due course we went and found the keeper all set to go. He warned us, however, that unless the wind abated, it would certainly not be possible to go out in the boat. It was, he said, a flat-bottomed affair and quite beyond his handling in the gale that was still blowing.

As we climbed up to the flat top which led across the moor to the loch we seemed to plunge into masses of rain-filled clouds. I had not come prepared for such weather, and it was not long before I was uncomfortably wet. My misery would have been complete but for a remark of the keeper. I commented that I had always understood fishing was useless when clouds and mist hung on the tops as they were now doing.

"This loch," said he, "is gey queer. I nivver can tell what's goin' tae happen till the flies are on the watter."

We arrived at the boathouse before noon, a more miserable and uninviting place I have never seen. Only a little of the loch was visible and that was a heaving mass of white-topped waves. The bit we could see was a narrow bay which was catching the full force of the wind. To take a flat-bottomed boat out was obviously out of the question.

Here I may record that, when I got a proper view of the loch, I saw nothing of beauty. It lies in the middle of a long shallow depression, about 900 feet above sea level; and there is not a tree or bush anywhere near it. It is not more than a mile long, with a maximum width of half a mile. To the south the loch is reed lined; otherwise its shores are mostly rough grass, and not noticeably peaty—a point, I think, of some importance. The water is not dark and peat coloured as hill lochs so often are. Several small flat islands just appear above its surface, and the depth varied from three to something like ten feet, the bottom being weed covered.

It was not until 2 p.m. that the keeper announced "the wind's easing" so up went the rods.

Here you should be told that my friend had never fished before; it was only for my sake he had engineered and accepted this invitation. The keeper was to look after him; I was to concentrate on catching fish!

By 2.30 we were afloat; by 2.31 the boathouse was out of sight in the mist; by 2.35. I was playing my first fish!

The wind settled to a steadiness which made fishing quite comfortable and by four o'clock the clouds broke, the mist rolled away, and the sun came out. Up to then trout rose steadily, and as if they meant to have the fly; but as soon as the sun got out, the rise began to tail off and I began to miss quite a few fish. My friend was rising a fair number of fish but somehow could not get the hook into them. Only one or two hung on, to use his own expression.

We went in at 6 p.m., and when the catch was counted they numbered twenty-five and the weight was fourteen pounds and a few ounces. I was very satisfied; my friend was delighted; the keeper took it all for granted.

There were, however, one or two noteworthy points about the catch. I did not catch one fish too small to keep, and the twenty-five appeared to be exactly the same size. Twenty-four of them were also alike in appearance, and obviously of the Loch Leven strain which had been introduced two or three times during the previous twenty years; but one trout was quite different from all the others. As they lay on the grass the difference was remarkable.

It was dark on the back, and lightening through olive on the flanks to yellow on the belly. It was spotted or rather blotched with black marks but had no red spots at all. The fish was, in fact, more like a Gillaroo, both in colour and shape, than any I have seen since the last one I saw from the loch of that name in Sutherland.

The keeper pointed it out as a pure "native". We kept it separate in the cooking and found the flesh nearer red than pink. It had almost the flavour of salmon. So, I remarked, *that* was the trout much favoured of anglers nearly a century ago; I am not surprised. What a pity, indeed, that the breed has been crossed. I like Loch Leven, and have no fault whatever to find with *Salmo Levenensis,* but the native of the Loch of the Showers was surely a breed worth keeping pure.

This first visit took place in July 1945. I went again in July 1946. This was a dull day with a light breeze from the S.E. It seemed a reasonably good day for loch fishing. I fished hard for seven hours. I caught only eighteen and the weight was a bare 9 lb. Once again they were all the same size; but there was not one native amongst them.

I anticipated my third visit; which was to take place in July 1947; but there came a queer twist in my fortunes. The invitation was forthcoming, and had been accepted; but on the appointed day I was helpless with a broken collarbone and ribs.

Before July 1948 I was again fit, ready, and as full of hope as ever. But, alas! There was no invitation.

Now, I am wondering, shall I ever fish the Loch of the Showers again?

CASTING AT FALKIRK

FROM reports received, it is clear that the Casting Tournament which took place at Callendar House Lake, Falkirk, on July 28, aroused so much interest that a casting club or association is to be formed in Falkirk.

According to a Scottish Press account, local anglers using orthodox fishing tackle maintained a commendably high standard of casting, and the large audience enjoyed greatly a, to them, novel type of sporting event. During the evening demonstrations were given by J. E. May, Monsieur Pierre Creusevaut and Captain T. L. Edwards, all of whom are casters of international repute.

We understand that this successful venture was organized by Mrs K. L. Scrimgeour, of Falkirk, and her committee. We congratulate all concerned and wish them well in their future undertakings.

The ⅝-oz. bait-casting event in progress during the casting tournament at Falkirk

PHOTO HINT No 8

UNCOMFORTABLE WADERS

COMES the time when in an emergency, many an angler welcomes the loan of a pair of gum-boots or rubber thigh-waders, which are "a world too wide for his shrunk shanks".

Should this be your lot, or if your own Wellingtons are uncomfortably roomy, try the tip illustrated here. By this simple expedient you can eliminate that looseness which so quickly produces chafing and painful blisters.

All you need are two lengths of soft cord or pliable rope. It has been known for a well-used clothes-line to shrink suddenly and mysteriously, but don't mention it in domestic circles.

Having procured these simple ingredients carry them firmly under the insteps once and twice round the ankles and *hey presto*, you have comfort.

A simple device to prevent chafing

Salmon Poaching in Southern Scotland

By J. F. HAMPTON

POACHING has become a menace to salmon fishing in Southern Scotland, especially in small rivers like the Doon and Ayr. Even at its mouth, the Doon is only 25 yards wide, and except for holding pools which vary considerably in depth, it is a shallow river. The gravel bottom is comparatively free from large boulders, and artificial obstructions, such as stakes driven into the river bed, are removed by the poachers before the river is drawn.

They work at night. First searchers inspect every bush and piece of cover near the river which it has been arranged to "draw", to ensure that no one will observe the netting. Then, the poachers, crawling on all fours, arrive with their nets. They know that sky lines are not only on the hill tops. These poachers work silently, the splashing of a salmon caught in the net being the only noise from their operations. The net is held at one end on the bank, then taken out across the river and back in a wide arc. Two or three draws are often made in a night. The results are most destructive to a fishery, especially when the fish are in the lower reaches of the river and there is insufficient water to entice them over the passes. A haul of 20 salmon in a night is not unusual and it is easy to make £50 for such a catch.

Those deep rocky pools which are unsuitable for netting are cleared by explosives. Pools near railway bridges are often the scene of this type of damage. The poachers await the arrival of a train and as it crosses the bridge, fire the charge so covering the noise of the explosion. The fish which are stunned and always die can be picked out of the river easily down stream. I have seen fish which have been killed by this terrible method: in every case they were very light in colour, the explosive having some peculiar effect on the pigmentation. Fish killed in this way never stiffen but are always flabby.

In the majority of cases the poachers work in organised gangs; one in South Ayrshire has inflicted great damage and is known generally as the Maybole gang because, apparently, its headquarters are somewhere in that neighbourhood. Some of the fish are possibly getting into the hands of legitimate fishmongers, in which case, the Ministry of Food apparently has the power, under S.R.O. 1784 of September 1st, 1942, Fish Licensing of Dealers Order, to take action.

In the Loch Lomond area poachers use a deeper type of net.

The River Leven is about ten miles long and connects Loch Lomond with the River Clyde. It is the only channel up which migratory fish can pass between the sea and the whole of the Loch Lomond drainage area. Despite the poacher's efficient intelligence and scouting service a large number of convictions are obtained. In addition to these numbers of nets have been confiscated:—

1942	17 nets
1943	16 nets
1944	6 nets to June 1

Salmon ladder on the Lower Doon, Ayrshire

It is to be regretted that the penalties, even after conviction by a Court of Law, are quite inadequate under present conditions.

Poachers may be charged with Day Poaching under the Salmon Fisheries (Scotland) Act, 1828, which reads as follows:—

Section 3 (1828) "If any person shall trespass in any ground, enclosed or unenclosed, or in or upon any river, stream, watercourse or estuary, with intent to kill salmon, grilse, sea trout, or other fish of the salmon kind, such person shall forfeit and pay any sum not less than ten shillings, and not exceeding five pounds."

Section 1 of the 1844 Act reads:—

"If any person, not having a legal right or permission from the proprietor of the salmon fishery, shall wilfully take, fish for, or attempt to take, in or from any river, stream, lake, water, estuary, firth, creek, bay or shore of the sea, or in or upon any part of the sea, within one mile of low-water mark in Scotland, any salmon, grilse, sea trout, whitling, or other fish of the salmon kind, such person shall forfeit and pay a sum not less than ten shillings and not exceeding five pounds for each and every such offence and shall, if the Sheriff or Justices shall think proper, over and above forfeit each and every fish so taken, and each and every boat, boat tackle, net, or other engine used in taking, fishing for, or attempting to take fish as aforesaid, and it shall be lawful for any person employed in the execution of this Act to seize and detain all fish so taken, and all boats, tackle, nets and other engines so used, and to give information thereof to the Sheriff or any Justice of the Peace, and any Sheriff or Justice may give such orders concerning the immediate disposal of the same as may be necessary."

Prosecution must follow within six months of the offence.

If the offence was committed at night, then the provisions of 1862 will apply.

Section 27, 1862, Act—

"If three or more persons, acting in concert, or being together or in company, shall at any time between the expiration of the first hour after sunset on any day and the beginning of the last hour before sunrise on the following morning, enter or be found upon any ground adjacent or near to any river or estuary of the sea, with intent illegally to take or kill salmon or having in his or their possession any net, rod, spear, light or other instrument used for taking salmon, every such person shall be guilty in Scotland of a criminal offence, and shall, for every such offence, be liable to a fine not exceeding five pounds, or to imprisonment for any period not exceeding three months."

In addition, poachers may often be charged with failing to comply with the weekly close time for nets, i.e. from 6 p.m. on Saturday until 6 a.m. on Monday, or failing to comply with provisions regulating the mesh of a salmon net, which must be a minimum of 1¾ inches from knot to knot or 7 inches round each mesh.

ANGLING, Summer No. 36, Vol. VIII, will appear on June 22.

North of the Border—III
FRUSTRATED BY DROUGHT
by W. A. Adamson

IN Britain it is folly to complain of fine weather. Heat-waves are excellent for children's holidays and give comely young women a rare chance to wear sunsuits. Nobody has ever met a satisfied or enthusiastic farmer, of course, but if these master grousers have not made hay while the sun shone in their rabbitless Edens, they have only themselves to blame, for there was no rain worthy of the name in Scotland during July and the first half of August.

Strange reports are appearing in the newspapers. Sea trout and grilse have been seen rising off shore in most unlikely places. No doubt they are puzzled and wandering up and down the coast while waiting for fresh water. One must sympathize with those anglers who try to time their annual fortnight to coincide with the cream of the sea trout fishing in July. They were dealt a cruel blow, but at least one of them is reported to have done well.

The story comes from the Ythan at Newburgh. It seems that an angler from the South resorted to coarse-fishing technique and "baited his swim" lavishly with maggot while using conventional float-tackle. He made an excellent basket of sea trout, and one cannot but admire his resourcefulness and also his nerve in braving the taunts of more conventional anglers. Exceptional circumstances demand ingenuity and versatility, but it would never do if this kind of thing were to become general!

Cats Welcome Record Chub
When Dr. Cameron of Dumfries hooked a heavy fish on his Brown Turkey fly in the Rotchell pool of the Annan, he was disappointed to find that he had merely caught Britain's record chub, weighing 10¼ lb. It is believed that several cats belonging to a lady who lives in the neighbourhood were mistakenly under the impression that this was "just what the doctor ordered".

It is to be regretted that this fine fish did not fall to some English angler who would have known how to appreciate it. In recent years Scotland has produced a pike of 47 lb. 11 oz. and a grayling of 7 lb. 2 oz.; both are records for the United Kingdom. Is there, I wonder, such a thing as a six-pound perch in Scotland? It may be that climate and competition combine to make this unlikely, but on the other hand nobody fishes seriously for big perch north of Tweed, although there are several waters known to contain them. The pressure on English coarse fisheries has been slightly eased by a mutually beneficial traffic of anglers to Eire. Judging by these records, Scotland ought to attract coarse fishers also. A Sassenach invasion of record-seekers would be welcomed if it materially reduced our population of chub, perch and pike.

A Royal Perch
I think most anglers would agree that our royal family should be enabled to enjoy as much "private" life as possible. Nevertheless it is possible to sympathize with the Press when it succumbs to the temptation to afford us some charming glimpses of the endearing personality of Princess Anne. Shortly before her fifth birthday she went fishing in Galloway

and caught a small perch. Later, she was overheard to call out from the deck of the *Britannia* to two young friends who had come to see her leave. With the polite solicitude which becomes an experienced angler, she was heard to inquire, "Did *you* catch any fish?"

More Scope For Scottish Anglers

"What Scotland needs is half-a-dozen Loch Levens!" John Kerr Hunter, of the Council of Physical Recreation, produced that remark, and I confess it shook me considerably. I hastened to explain that Loch Leven was the unique product of peculiarly favourable natural resources coupled with years of skilful management. On talking things over, however, I had to agree that there were a great many waters in Scotland which could easily be greatly improved in order to give a great deal more fishing to many more anglers. The Lake of Menteith used to be a good trout water before the pike took over once more; Loch Lubnaig cries out for restoration and even Vennachar and Achray could be made to yield first-class and very convenient sport. Pike present no problem nowadays and expert advice and assistance could easily be obtained. We have seen how the Hydro-electric Board turned over a first-class fishing to Pitlochry. When is the Forestry Commission going to do something about Loch Morlich and Loch Lubnaig?

That is not the real answer, of course. The trouble lies not in our stars but in ourselves. We do not want the responsibility, we do not want the work involved, and above all, we do not want to pay for our sport! Otherwise there would appear to be no reason why, let us say, a large association of Glasgow anglers should not begin the arduous task of investigating the legal position with a view to acquiring rights from riparian proprietors at Lubnaig or elsewhere.

A.C.A. Members in Scotland

But before I doze off into this dreamworld I am creating, let us drink a draught of grim realism. The following figures give a good idea of how reluctant Scottish anglers are to dip into their pockets in the cause of angling. Here is a breakdown of the Scottish Membership of the Anglers' Co-operative Association.

County	Number of Members	Population	Members per 100,000
Aberdeenshire	33	329,900	10.0
Angus	68	275,000	24.7
Argyll	5	58,800	8.6
Ayr	23	326,400	7.0
Banff	17	50,900	33.4
Berwick	7	24,600	28.4
Caithness	1	23,800	4.1
Clackmannan	1	39,000	2.6
Dumfries	6	88,000	7.0
Dumbarton	12	167,000	7.1
East Lothian	3	51,900	5.8
Fife	14	314,300	4.4
Inverness	6	84,700	7.1
Kincardine	1	28,000	3.6
Kinross	1	7,300	13.6
Kirkcudbright	–	29,800	–
Lanark	49	1,617,100	3.0
Midlothian	76	573,500	13.3
Moray	10	50,200	20.0
Nairn	1	8,400	11.9
Peebles	–	14,400	–
Perth	30	127,100	23.6
Renfrew	26	329,700	7.9
Ross and Cromarty	1	59,500	1.7
Roxburgh	23	45,300	50.8
Selkirk	4	21,200	19.0
Stirling	8	189,800	4.2
Sutherland	2	13,000	15.4
West Lothian	1	91,100	1.1
Wigtown	5	30,400	16.4
Islands	8	56,800	14.1
Total	442	5,127,800	8.6
England and Abroad	9		
Grand total	451		

TRACING THE KENMURE SKULL
by Michael Logan

THE following story of a missing head, of a search and a discovery, concerns what is perhaps the most famous fish in piscatorial history.

Two years ago, ANGLING published a letter under the heading "Where are they?" (ANGLING No. 73, Vol. XIII, page 684). The writer recalled the famous Kenmure pike, which is probably the best authenticated of the super-monsters of British pike-lore, and mentioned that the head of this great fish was generally supposed to be at Kenmure Castle. So, seized with consuming curiosity, I visited the Castle, only to find that the head was not there; and that no one could tell me where it was.

Further correspondence followed,

Kenmure Castle and Loch Ken, Kirkcudbrightshire

which gave some interesting details of the fish. But no one, so far as I know, has come forward with any information regarding the whereabouts of the much discussed skull of this pike.

I was, moreover, curious, not only as to the fate of this relic but also about the present-day inhabitants of Loch Ken; and this year, armed with a stout rod, I took an autumn holiday in Galloway. Kenmure Castle was a comfortable base from which to begin both the pursuit of live pike and my hunt for the remains of a dead monster.

Let us follow the trail to its vanishing point. What do we know about the history of this great fish? We know that it existed, who caught it, and that the eminent ichthyologist, the late Dr C. Tate Regan, measured its skull and proclaimed it a veritable giant among pike. For the rest, its weight has been variously reported as 61 and 72 lb. Even the bait which lured it to its doom is in dispute. The popular version says that it was a fly with a peacock wing; yet another says that it was caught by spinning; and a Galloway antiquarian claims that the bait was a waterfowl.

To support those who believe the Loch Ken pike was caught on a fly, is there not the reproduction of a painting of the head together with the rod, gaff and fly that caught it, which appeared in ANGLING No. 79, Vol. XIV, page 355, as well as the details of the fly? This painting was signed "W. Meikle, Walsall 1897".

If this was the date when the picture was painted, it would appear, to say the least, that a little artistic licence was taken. The head in this picture was clothed in flesh and the eye stared reproachfully at the beholder. But could there have been either flesh or an eye remaining in 1897? Writing of this same fish in 1879 (eighteen years earlier), Houghton in his *British Freshwater Fishes* said he was told: "The head has lost some of its bones and in consequence looks smaller than it used to." And when Tate Regan measured it in about 1910, it was definitely a skeleton and he stated that the occipital region of the skull was missing.

According to local legend, this monster did much to vindicate the honour of John Murray, who caught it sometime in the 1760's. Murray, who was keeper at Kenmure, had the task of catching fish for the table; and after a long run of undersized trout had been forthcoming, his master remarked that the loch now contained nothing but parr. There was no doubt some warmth in Murray's reply, when he threw down the great fish exclaiming "Does your lordship ca' that a minnen?"

The tombstone of John Murray in the churchyard of Kells. The emblems are a powder-horn, fishing rod, gun, hound and partridge.

Murray was an allround sportsman and a remarkable character. His tombstone in the parish churchyard of Kells bears on its sandstone face the device of a fishing rod, gun, hound, partridge and powder-horn. It states that he died in 1777 and on its reverse I found this wistful epitaph.

Ah John what changes since I saw thee last;
Thy fishing and thy shooting days are past.
Bagpipes and hautboys thou canst sound no more;
Thy nods, grimaces, wink and pranks are o'er.
Thy harmless, queerish incoherent talk,
Thy wild vivacity and trudging walk
Will soon be quite forgot. Thy joys on earth—
A snuff, a glass, riddles and noisy mirth—
Are vanished all. Yet blest I hope thou art
For in thy station, well thou play'dst thy part.

It is known that the skull of Murray's great pike remained in the library at Kenmure Castle until well into the present century, and then, between the two wars, the castle changed hands, and has since had several occupiers. When the first change of ownership took place, the skull left the castle. I believe that it had several resting places thereafter, although it remained the property of the family who had owned Kenmure.

After the second world war a member of this family lived in the neighbourhood of New Galloway, and the skull was in his possession until he left the place a few years ago. It was from this point that my trail grew indistinct.

I talked with several people who remembered it. Some said it was here, some that it was there; but the general version seemed to be that its owner,

Mr Maitland-Gordon, had taken it away with him.

A pike, even a large one, arouses little enthusiasm and even less reverence North of the Border. Everybody was surprisingly calm about the fate of this curiosity. Then, after much speculation and enquiry, a resident with whom I had discussed the mystery several times said in the frame a disappointingly slight, yellowish object reposed, which bristled with teeth. Was this the skull for which I had sought diligently?

Closer examination showed why its size was unimpressive. Little more than a pair of enormous jaw bones remained to the upper of which two narrow fragments of the top of the skull were still

Skull of the Kenmure Pike photographed on September 16, 1952

he believed that this unique skull was still in the neighbourhood, and he had a theory as to who might have it.

I persuaded him to follow this up and a day later he confirmed that what remained of the skull had been left by its owner for safe keeping with one of the local cottagers, who had placed it in an outhouse.

When I called in the afternoon of the same day, I was shown a dusty case from which most of the glass was missing. It was perched on a wooden box in the semi-darkness of the outhouse. Within- attached. The total length of these remains was $9\frac{1}{2}$ ins. There was nothing to identify the bones, but this was obviously part—a very small part—of what must have been a gigantic pike.

Unhappily, I had no note of the portions which the late Dr Tate Regan had measured and my measurements could not, therefore, be compared with his. The jaw was 6 ins. across and the toothed portion of the lower jaw, measured in a straight line, was $6\frac{1}{2}$ ins. long. This does not, however convey the full length of jaw in its original state. Regan found this to be $8\frac{3}{4}$ ins. The teeth in the lower jaw were amazingly long. Some of them, including the protruding portions of the bony sockets, were an inch in length.

The general effect was to me somewhat disappointing, partly because my lay eye could not visualize the missing portions and still less the original dimensions of the living head. Here again I must quote Tate Regan, who estimated that the full length of the head was probably over 13 ins.—and the head of a pike is often relatively small in relation to the rest of its body.

The case which housed the remains measured $15 \times 9 \times 10$ ins. and appeared to be relatively modern. I should say that it was made sometime during last century. The lower jaw was roughly nailed to the base of this case, on which some fragments of disconnected bone were scattered; and the wiring which held the upper and lower jaws together had rusted through and broken.

Readers will, I think, share my hope as this famous relic was locked once more in that outhouse, that this will not be the end of the story.

North of the Border—VIII
THE HYDRO-ELECTRIC CONTROVERSY by W. A. Adamson

SEVERAL Scottish newspapers have commented on a very forthright editorial in a contemporary angling monthly attacking hydro-electric schemes for their effect on salmon. Are Scottish salmon being exterminated or even materially reduced by hydro-electric activities?

Many anglers find it hard to be strictly fair in their judgements on this question, and all anglers know how extremely difficult it is to arrive at the truth of the matter. It is late in the day, indeed, to agitate for a reversal of policy. Rightly or wrongly, it was decided more than twenty years ago that our requirements of power were paramount and that the schemes should be put through. It is known too that the Galloway and Shannon schemes most certainly had a temporarily adverse effect on the salmon runs.

Fishery Committees have been set up for each scheme, and endless trouble has been taken to minimise interference with migration and spawning. We have had the benefit of American and European experience in such measures, and, although it may seem hard to believe that a smolt which has gone backwards through a turbine can ever be the same again, it is many years since unbiassed observers confirmed the robust resilience of the tiny fish by protracted experiment.

Of course, many and ingenious devices are employed with the object of ensuring that fish do not go through the turbines, and that they are diverted and protected from harm. How far such methods go towards success, and how far the enormous losses of smolts in "natural" conditions are increased by hydro-electric obstacles and "accidents" is by no means easy to determine.

As an example of the difference of opinion which may exist about vital statistics for Scottish salmon, compare the view of Mr. K. A. Pyefinch that salmon stocks appear to have shown no marked decline over the years (suggesting that netsmen might well take more fish than they do at present) with this other suggestion that Scottish salmon face extermination.

Only a churl would refuse to acknowledge the sincerity and good intention of the hydro-electric people or the eminence and authority of the experts they employ. The work done at the Brown Trout Research Laboratory (maintained and financed partly by the hydro-electric Board) and at Lochs Poulary and at Contin is designed to increase fishing facilities and to make new spawning grounds and salmon rivers where none existed before.

Every angler must regret that the Perthshire Garry is now reduced pitifully in volume, but the adjacent main road in Drumouchter made this a poacher's paradise at the best of times.

From the angler's point of view an accurate balance-sheet of losses and gains would be hard to draw up, but if one wanted to make odious comparisons they would not be hard to find. There appears to be no hope for the future of salmon in the Forth, and that unhappy situation cannot be laid at the door of hydro-electric development. The entire salmon fishings of the Clyde sell for a token payment of five pounds per annum, and who is to blame for that? Is not pollution at all times the greater menace? A recent hydro-electric project involves the comparatively short river Awe, which is not very far from Glasgow and roughly one third of the entire population of Scotland. This fact may account for the present revival of criticism of hydro-electric activity, but the crusaders of 1956 are mounted on the corpses of horses which were flogged to death years ago, and what they say now has been said often before. In reviving the controversy, there is an inference that had it not been for the hydro-electric people, everything in the garden would be lovely. Yet the Board is one of the few bodies that have done anything to promote the interests of anglers. In angling, as in life, nobody can get more out of it than they are prepared to put into it. The cry for free fishing, for cheap fishing, for better fishing, or for the moderation of abuses is raised all too often nowadays in the complete absence of any plan for action or for sacrifices of money or time by anglers themselves. Reformers must be prepared to back their words with deeds.

Lochs and Lakes Compared

The Scottish angler is immeasurably better off than his English neighbour. In writing that I am poaching in a literary and geographic sense, but the comparison is interesting. About a month ago I made a border raid into the English Lake District. Here, one might have thought, the English could have concentrated effort to develop fisheries comparable with the best anywhere. There is good fishing to be had, but how much better might it not be made?

Blagdon is renowned in a way which no water in Cumberland or Westmorland can rival. Blagdon, of course, is under the complete administration of one body. The lakes of the north-west are subject to many conflicting interests. A storm of protest was raised when the traditional free fishing on Ullswater was threatened some years ago. Much of the fishing that took place there was a little too "free", and therein may lie part of the difficulty. There is competition between game and coarse fishers and, while it would seem unfair to restrict coarse fishing, coarse fishers must inevitably catch trout inadvertently by means not usually accounted suitable for trout. Yet the elimination of coarse fish to improve game fishing would scarcely be tolerated. This sort of difficulty seldom arises in Scotland.

To indulge in pipe dreams about the possibilities of improving any fishery is a fascinating pastime, but sooner or later one must ask, where are the necessary funds to be obtained? That problem lies at the root of every plan for improvement, and the angler must nearly always pay for such improvement in the long run.

Snow and Salmon

Can spring be far behind? In the first week of January it appeared to have arrived in Scotland. To a smog-bound Southron I had just written a gloating letter of commiseration describing a mild sunny day full of birdsong and the suggestion of growth and buds. Alas, gales and blizzards supervened overnight. Snow does not prevent a piper leading the trollers to Loch Tay where, with typically Scottish prodigality, a bottle of whisky must be shattered on the bows of the boat. At Tweed-mouth the waters are ceremoniously blessed with benefit of clergy. Chill Loch Ness is monstrously attractive to the devotee, and a new salmon season begins.

Memories of International Day on Loch Leven

By "ZULU"

[*Space has been accorded to commentaries on coarse fishing matches in this journal and similar facilities will be given again. This time we are glad to record the impressions of an international competitor in the famous Loch Leven trout fishing match.*—ED.]

INTERNATIONAL day on Loch Leven is the greatest event of the year on that far-famed water. That day you will find chosen representatives of England, Scotland, Ireland and Wales trying conclusions with the wily trout and with each other, all for the glory of their country and for the honour of holding the Montgomery Cup.

A spirit of healthy rivalry prevails. The sport is the thing. Competition is keen as could be, but it is clean and open. Nothing deceitful or underhand is ever attempted. Any of your rivals will be only too pleased to tell you where he found the trout the previous day and to name the successful flies.

Activities commence a day or two before the match. A couple of days' experience on the Loch is of inestimable value. On the eve of the big day each team holds a meeting, when the captain imparts his last words of advice, tactics for various weather conditions are discussed, and flies, proved that day to be " the goods," are passed round for examination—so to bed.

We are early astir in the morning. Our first thought is of the weather, one glance through the window is sufficient to confirm our most gloomy forebodings. Not a leaf is stirring. After a hurried scrape, we arrive at the breakfast-table only to have our worst fears confirmed. Several members of our team have been down to the Loch, and there is a heart-breaking monotony in their reports—" surface like oil "—" not a suspicion of a ripple "—" utterly hopeless," etc.

However, we recall that conditions are the same for all, and extract cold comfort from the fact. Breakfast is hurried and at 8.45 we assemble on the pier. The casts already in our dampers are allowed to remain there, and we descend in a body on the two tackle shops so conveniently at hand. Here we acquire a stock of smaller flies on lighter casts. Then, of course, we must pose for a battery of cameras, amateur and professional. The pier

The race for position commences

by this time is a seething mass of humanity. All Kinross seems to be there.

As each pair of anglers comes forward their boatmen are allotted by the officer in charge, who has been supplied with the allocation details the previous night. Each boatman attaches himself to an angler. He takes charge of all the accessories—spare rod, casts, oilskins, seats, bass (for the trout, Mr. Editor), and lunch-box (including Bass for the angler!). He will assemble the rod to be used, unless the nervous angler has already done so. If asked, he will advise certain flies for use, and his advice is well worth having. Take my tip, and leave everything to him. He appreciates your confidence, and will do all in his power to ensure you a successful day.

Memories of International Day on Loch Leven

Now, walk slowly down the pier. Cinematographers are here in force, so you must assume an attitude of confidence, spiced with a demeanour, " if, by any freak of fortune, we do not win, at least we can take our beating like gentlemen."

As 9.30 (zero hour) approaches, there is a general move towards the boats moored on either side of the little pier. You take a hurried look round the boat to see that nothing is forgotten, and then step aboard. The boatman in the stern unties the painter which remains attached to the pier, but holds it in his hand. He must not let go before the stroke of 9.30, which comes at last.

The flag falls and the scramble to get away commences. The boats have been moored three or four feet apart, but the oars must be at least 16 feet long, and every boat is determined to be first out. Bumping, boring, pulling and hauling, it is accomplished somehow, the oars are placed in the rowlocks, and the race for position begins. I am bow rod, so it is hopeless for me to attempt to fish, particularly as trolling one's flies is prohibited. Stern rod, however, starts fishing at once, as it is quite common to hook trout on Loch Leven, even when the boat is being rowed quite rapidly. Stern perseveres throughout the row out, but not a single rise rewards him.

I should mention here that the boats on Loch Leven are 18 to 20 feet long—sound, safe craft. Each boatman uses one oar only, quite enough for any man. He works it in a long steady sweep, and the time is perfect. The boats skim over the surface of the Loch, each making for the same " grounds "—those broad Shallows at the eastern end, about three miles from Kinross.

Looking back, we can see Kinross House, home of the late Lady Graham Montgomery, the donor of the International Cup. An historic mansion, it was at one

FOSTERS'
"CAMOUFLAGED" GUT
(FULLY PROTECTED BY PATENT RIGHTS)

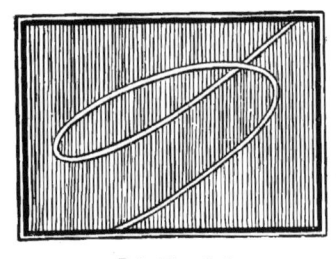

Pale Blue Gut

By its use you get the Fish that have turned all your previous advances down. Fish don't fight shy of it. They do not see its connection with your Fly. Try it and BE CONVINCED.

Camouflaged Trout Casts

Tapered Casts Camouflaged 1x to 3x, 4x and
5x ... ... 2 yds. **1/6**
3 yds. **2/2**
Tapered Casts Camouflaged Light Lake to
2x ... ... 2 yds. **1/9**
3 yds. **2/6**
Best Quality Undrawn Casts, Level, Stout,
Medium and Fine ... ... 2 yds. **1/6**
3 yds. **2/2**

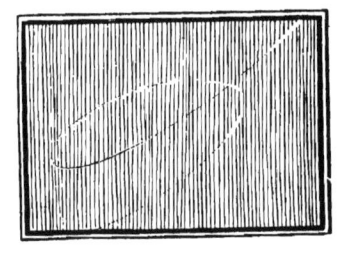

Camouflaged Gut

We are very jealous of the quality of our casts and a high standard of quality is being maintained, despite the acute shortage of best grade gut, owing to the trouble in Spain.

> "I used your Camouflaged Casts last season; the results obtained are by no means exaggerated, but **rather the reverse.** I cannot understand how any angler can continue to use the old-fashioned casts when the Camouflaged ones are available. I have just examined my last year's casts, and find them in excellent condition."
> Exeter.
> (Signed) J. HARVEY BAINS.

Anglers' Guide and Catalogue post free 4d. Anglers' Exchange 2d.

FOSTER BROS.
Gold Medal Fishing Tackle Manufacturers

MIDLAND WORKS, ASHBOURNE :: Telephone No. Ashbourne 135

Memories of International Day on Loch Leven

time owned by James II when he was Duke of York. Our course takes us between two of the many islands which stud the Loch, Castle Island and Reed Bower. It is impossible to pass the former, actually within a stone's throw of the walls of the grim old castle, without bestowing a thought on it. It was in its heyday in 1335, when Edward III tried to take it, but failed. It is still better remembered, however, as the place of imprisonment of the unhappy Mary, Queen of Scots, from which she escaped on May 2nd, 1568. While it is safe to surmise that not one of the competitors on the bosom of the Loch would exchange Mary's regal crown for a record basket of trout, yet the faint voice of our history (and faint it is!) serves to bring us back to the business in hand, as it is recorded by Sir Walter Scott that while the ill-fated Queen was a prisoner there, young Roland Grahame fished for trout at the west point of Castle Island.

During the long, long row across the Loch, a very gentle zephyr-like breeze steals over the surface of the water. At once we feel more hopeful. The boat is turned broadside on to it, and we get going. All the other boats are either fishing or preparing to fish. No boat may come within 100 yards of any other, but there is room for all. We fished two long slow drifts on the Shallows, but not a rise did we get. Indeed, as our boatmen told us, but one fish was caught by any boat on those two drifts. Those boatmen can see every fish netted within a radius of at least two miles, and not a semblance of a rise in the path of their own boat passes unnoticed.

Discouraged, we decided to try the northern portion of the Loch, leaving the other boats becalmed on the Shallows. This seems reasonable, but the thought that the others know better is always present, and that you are leaving the known for the unknown. We fretted at

"Zulu"

the time lost in rowing when we might be fishing, but kept on hoping that the new water would justify our decision.

We got among the rising trout all right, but it was a difficult matter to offer them something which they would accept. The breeze, such as it was, died away completely at 12.30, and with it all our hopes of record baskets. At this time we had two fish in the boat, one each. We fished on and on, cast following monotonous cast. Stern rod mounted a dry fly, but without success. He reverted to wet, and then for a few minutes the trout came on the feed, during which time we each netted two.

All too soon it was over, but we, poor devils, had to keep on in a flat calm, hoping against hope, keep on while we snatched a hasty lunch, keep on till we cursed Loch Leven, the International Match and everything connected with it.

We didn't win, but we learnt a lot.

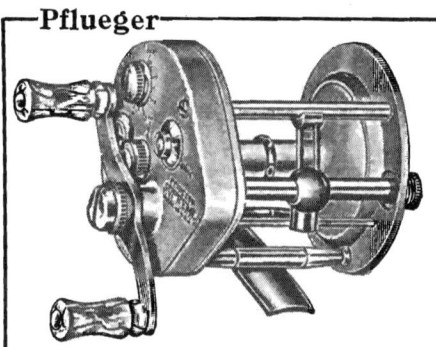

Pflueger

"Supreme"—
the
ultimate reel
£6/7/6

Under rod model:
£9/12/6

ASK for pocket catalogue

Fulsome "blurb" cannot convey an adequate idea of its perfection — TRY ONE!

Sole concessionaires: Wholesale only

Modern Arms Co. Ltd.
58 Southwark Bridge Road
London, S.E.1

SEA-FISHING IN ROSS-SHIRE
by Wanderer

WHEN the question of a sea-fishing holiday is mooted, I have found it profitable to overlook the more popular and over-fished stations and to go further afield in search of the less known and unspoiled venues which are still available.

There is for example a great deal of first-class sea-fishing on the West Coast of Scotland. My favourite venues are in Ross-shire, and without doubt the best of them is Shieldaig.

A fishing station is known by its results and Shieldaig has produced prize-winning specimens consistently since it was, so to speak, discovered by Cecil Copping, then Commodore of the Dreadnought Sea Angling Society, 20 years ago.

Shieldaig is a tiny off-the-beaten-track fishing station composed of a few whitewashed cottages where the sea runs up almost to their front doors and towering cliffs and mountains complete the scene.

It rivals Eire's Ballycotton for large bags and falls short of the Irish station only in that it has no well-appointed hotels; and Alec Cameron is the only boatman who really caters for anglers. But what accommodation there is with the villagers is good and the food is excellent.

As Ballycotton is noted for large skate, halibut, shark and ling so Shieldaig is famous for its whiting, coalfish, cod, gurnard, dabs and haddock. The world record whiting, which weighed 6 lb., came from Shieldaig and was caught by my friend, Ernie Tame. Whiting weighing 4 lb. are fairly common. Last year I caught a hundredweight and a half of whiting and haddock in four hours, and six of the whiting weighed more than 4 lb. each.

One fishes in two arms of the sea, namely, Loch Torridon and Loch Shieldaig. The whiting, dabs and haddock seem to prefer Torridon, particularly that portion known as Inner Torridon, while coalfish, cod, conger, gurnard, mackerel and pollack abound in Shieldaig. Throughout both lochs there are plenty of dog fish, spotted, spur and black-mouthed, so much so that at times they can be a nuisance.

There is never any shortage of bait. One can fill a large bag with mussels or cockles in an hour; and for a little searching supplies of razor fish and a good number of sand-eels can be collected.

Most of the best marks are in deep water, two in Torridon which are frequented by the large whiting and haddock are over 40 fathoms deep, and unless one's reel is equipped with large handles, aching fingers and wrist will certainly be the result.

Shieldaig "coalies" and a two-inch gold devon or large Alexandra fly is good medicine for the mackerel.

There is some excellent rock-fishing for pollack and conger round these two lochs. When spinning a devon for the pollack, sea-trout which hug the shore of the lochs are sometimes caught. It was while spinning for pollack some years ago that I landed a 9¼ lb. sea-trout which was followed by three others, all of which weighed over 3 lb.

For the angler who is also a bird-

A 4½ lb. whiting with haddock, spur dog and mackerel from Loch Torridon

A three-boomed paternoster is the best whiting tackle, but the snoods should be fairly stout as quite often large cod take hold. Twice last year I had two whiting on the top hooks and a 14 lb. cod on the bottom simultaneously. The heaviest rod-caught cod from here weighed 27 lb. and was taken by Cecil Copping.

In midsummer the coalfish and mackerel come in and the angler whose visit coincides with their arrival is assured of some fine sport. Fourteen-pound coalfish are fairly common and the mackerel run to a good size, two-pounders being not uncommon. A 12-inch rubber eel is the best bait for the

lover, Shieldaig is second to none. Its avian population ranges from the lordly peregrine to the tiny goldcrest. There are gulls and terns of every description, eider-ducks, mallards, divers, mergansers, oyster-catchers, herons, guillemots, and occasionally one sees a skua robbing the gulls of their food.

To be honest, the journey to Shieldaig by rail is tiresome. One goes by express from Euston to Inverness, where it is necessary to change for the Strathcarron express; and from Strathcarron it is a 21 mile bus ride to Shieldaig. The journey by car is much more pleasant and the wonderful scenery through which one passes more than compensates for

Loch Shieldaig and a corner of the village of Shieldaig, Wester Ross

the 600 miles which must be covered from London.

If you go by road the best of this scenery is, in my opinion, at Glencoe. Glencoe is famous as the scene of the massacre of its hospitable and unsuspecting inhabitants by Government troops in 1692. Though narrow, the Glencoe valley has a good road that traverses scenery which is at once awe-inspiring in its wildness and perhaps more romantic than any other in the Highlands. On every side black rocks rise almost perpendicular to a height of over 2,000 feet; and for many miles Nature, the greatest sculptor of all, has carved forms, some of which are majestic, others whimsical.

There are several unnamed lochs in the vicinity of Glencoe which are full of trout that average three to the pound; and in one I discovered char.

But to return to sea angling, there are other good stations in Ross-shire, one such is Plockton at the mouth of Loch Carron, near the Kyle of Loch Alsh; here again the accommodation and boat facilities are very limited.

Most of the marks are in the region of 30 fathoms deep and a seven- or eight-inch reel is essential. Carron is long and narrow and at one point in the middle depths of over 140 fathoms have been recorded. It is studded with a number of small islands off which there are some excellent marks. One can expect to catch coalfish, cod, whiting, dabs and haddock.

Gairloch is another grand spot which is well worth a visit both for its fishing, which is nearly on a par with that of Shieldaig, and for its magnificent scenery. Accommodation is much more readily obtainable here than at the other two places to which I have referred.

Gairloch became quite prominent during the first World War as it was here that members of the British Cabinet with the Prime Minister held several meetings.

Last, but by no means least we have Ullapool which has always given my friends and myself good sport. This village was established by the British Fisheries Association in 1788, and there is plenty of good accommodation and excellent boatmen are available.

As I see it, until good roads are built in the Highlands and there is transport

A seven- or eight-inch reel is essential

to run on them, Ross-shire in particular will remain a sea-angler's paradise. It holds one world's record and it would not surprise me to learn at any time that others have been set up. Who knows, YOU may be the angler to do it, but like so many things which are most worthwhile you must go to some trouble to attain the grand fishing to which I have introduced you.

SCOTTISH LOWLAND FISHING
by "Alexandra"

TO many Englishmen, fishing in Scotland means long and difficult journeys, and the expenditure of much time and money. For them it would be a delightful experience, but they regard it as too difficult to plan, and, speaking generally, outside their scope.

They seem to be oblivious of the excellent fishing which is available in countless places between the Border and the industrial Edinburgh-Glasgow line. There must, however, be thousands of keen anglers who drive up to Scotland on business every year, between February and November, who never think of taking a rod and planning their visit to include a day's fishing. For them I make a few suggestions.

Taking the south-western area first, let us imagine you are motoring to Glasgow. For you the angling opportunities are splendid. Just after you cross the Border the Esk flows under the main

Spinning for sea-trout on the Annan near Lockerbie

road. This really fine salmon and sea-trout river is at its best from August onwards. Beats are available and grand sport is assured.

Then you have the River Annan, which, though not well enough known, is one of the most delightful rivers in Scotland. It is excellent for trout, sea-trout, herling and salmon; and can be fished conveniently either from Lockerbie on the main road, or from any of the hotels *en route*. The upper waters however are best reached from Moffat,

A pool on the Nith near Sanquhar

Once over the Beattock summit, the Great Clyde has its source. Here one can step over it, as it gurgles through the grass by the roadside.

At Crawford and Abington accommodation is good, the river is free, and the trout are plentiful and of good size. I do not suggest that big baskets are easily obtained, but a good fisherman will do well if he fishes fine, with very small, sparsely dressed flies.

The tributaries, Duneaton and the Douglas Water, are crossed by the main road, but, while free fishings which hold some good trout, they are overfished.

Lower down the Clyde the fishing is even better, the stretch at Hyndford Bridge near Lanark being excellent. In the lovely Clydesdale Valley, where the river winds through an orchard-lined gorge, the trout are of great size, and evening fishing is the best. This stretch of perfect scenery, from Lanark down to Hamilton, is almost unknown to visitors, who generally associate the Clyde with its very different appearance at Glasgow.

Westwards of this main route to Scotland is the southern coast, and there is good fishing in nearly all the rivers which run into Solway Firth. At Dumfries the Nith, from the town up to its headwaters, provides good trout and excellent salmon and sea-trout fishing in the autumn. It is a pleasant diversion to reach Glasgow by this route, following the St Pancras-St Enoch railway line, which runs through the pretty valley of the Nith.

Dumfries, Thornhill and Sanquhar are all places from which this fine river can be fished, and the distance to Glasgow from Carlisle by this route is very little more than by the Beattock route.

Westwards along the southern coast from the mouth of the Nith are the rivers Cree, Urr, Dee and Fleet, all of which offer good sport to anyone who can persuade his business to take him in this direction.

From Stranraer up the west coast, there is the Stinchar at Ballantrae, really excellent for salmon and sea-trout after a flood; and the Girvan, the Doon and the Ayr, all with fishable stretches.

Coming north to Edinburgh from Newcastle, the wise fisherman will set westwards, either by the Carter Bar or Wooler route, or up the Tweed from Berwick, rather than keep to the Great North Road. This leads to the Great Tweed Valley, and its fine fishing throughout the season. The salmon fishing is superb on the best beats near Kelso, if somewhat expensive. But the trout fishing is good and cheap. The Teviot is a fine river which joins the Tweed above Kelso; and the Whitadder, near Duns, is a good trout stream, which with plenty of water can be excellent.

The Leader, the Ale, the Jed and the Tyne are all Tweed tributaries which offer fair trout fishing, but most of them are now overfished.

For those who desire to keep to the main road up the coast, the Tyne at Haddington offers some wary trout. Sea trout are also caught between the mouth and the Cauld at Amisfield.

There, then, are some suggestions for those who would like to combine pleasure with business, or who cannot afford the time for a prolonged holiday on our northern waters. Many will be surprised to find how good this southern fishing can be, particularly for migratory fish; and also, how well the southern trout compare in weight with the often disappointing, if plentiful baskets obtained in the far north.

HAVE YOU FISHED THE YTHAN? by Maurice Hartley

FOR many years circumstances compelled me to live in an industrial area where a full business life restricted my fishing to odd days, apart, of course, from my annual holiday. If you are similarly situated this article may help you.

The attractions of pure air, sparkling water, beautiful scenery and healthy exercise are all part of an angler's enjoyment, but frankly these aesthetic pleasures are only incidental to the main object which is to fish—and what is more, to catch fish.

Thousands have arranged a fishing holiday and travelled great distances only to find that their hopes and expectations which had been built up for months are not realized. There are, of course, many causes of this such as bad weather, too much or too little water, wrongly timed visits, or even worse, submission to the lure of an over-optimistic advertisement.

The lower estuary of the Ythan, Aberdeenshire, at high tide. The sand dunes on the far bank are a favourite spinning venue and are known as "The Spinning Bank". The dark line (*middle distance*) is the near bank at low tide

Much experience of these difficult problems brought me to the river Ythan a few miles north of Aberdeen. Here the head of sea-trout in the estuary during the normal holiday months of July, August and September is truly prodigious. I have known occasions when the fish leaped, boiled and plunged in every directiom, as far as one could see.

The fish enter the estuary from June onwards, and seem to move up and down with each tide for three or four months. They do not run straight up into the fresh water, as they do in many rivers, and the fishing is usually at its best a few days either side of the spring tides.

Three methods of fishing are in general use.

Fly-fishing

A ten-foot sea-trout fly-rod is very suitable for use from the shores. And the Ythan Terror, of which there are two types, is the most successful lure. (See Fig. 1.) One has a silver body with blue and white feathers, which represents the herring fry, and the other a silver body with brown feathers, which is tied to represent a sand eel. These lures are made in sizes from 2 to 4 inches long, and it is advisable to use one of each type on a cast. It is my experience that a 2½- or 3-inch Terror is generally speaking the best size; but in either rough weather or when fishing very deep the largest size is more successful. Dusk and dawn are the best times for this fishing, although, when the weather is warm and the fish are near the surface, good baskets can often be taken during the day.

The ebbing tide, particularly the last three hours, fishes better than the flow, and the shallower waters on the edge

1. Ythan terrors. (*Above*) A 2½-inch herring-fry pattern. (*Below*) A 3-inch sand-eel pattern

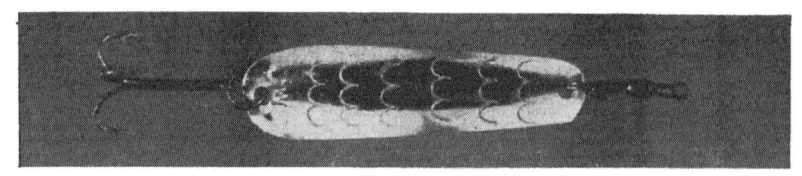

2. A typical 3-inch Ythan spoon

of the main stream, where small seaweed-covered islands appear as the tide recedes, usually hold taking fish. Ythan Terrors can either be obtained locally or can be made quite easily at home to the following recipe:

Three hooks are tied in tandem to the required length of twisted gut or wire, the tail hook being a double, and all hook-shanks are wrapped with plain or hammered silver tinsel. Four feathers are then tied in at the head and allowed to lie along the whole length, i.e. two blue and two white for the herring fry, and four brown or badger for the sand eel.

These lures are cast and worked in just the same manner as ordinary sea-trout flies.

Spinning

For spinning from the shore or bank, either a heavy trout or light grilse spinning outfit is quite suitable. Either a Silver, Blue and Silver or Silver and Red Devon, up to 2 inches long, a natural sand eel or an Ythan Spoon will be found taking. The latter, which is long and narrow, should be obtained locally. Although the ebb tide is the best for spinning, fish can be taken on the flow and even at slack water, by spinning slowly and deep.

Harling

Harling is, of course, carried out from rowing boats and it is usual to troll with a cast of two Terrors (one of each kind, spaced at 3-foot intervals) with a Ythan Spoon at the end. In this operation *it is most important* to keep your baits moving in steady jerks. This is done by pulling about a yard of line through the rings and then releasing it, and the movement should be made at the rate of sixty pulls to the minute; working the troll without this movement is practically useless. One can, of course, harl at any state of the tide; and boats and boatman may be hired locally. The local boatmen do not, for some reason, think much of anchoring a boat in the tideway and casting from it, but this can be very successful, especially when fish are showing on the surface.

The estuary fishing rights are privately owned, day tickets are, however, obtainable in the village of Newburgh; and an inquiry at the Post Office would elicit full details.

Ythan sea-trout average about 1½ lb. in weight, but there are many fish weighing from 2 to 3 lb. Among them even larger fish are frequently taken, and there is always an excellent chance of creeling a real grandfather. Two fine specimens of 14 and 18 lb. respectively look encouragingly from their cases in the hotel, the larger of which was taken quite recently. During my visits since the war a few fish of 4 to 6 lb. have been taken each week.

This fishing may lack the finesse of chalk-stream dry-fly fishing, but with suitably light tackle it provides excellent sport; and in the Ythan estuary *you do catch fish!*

A Scots Angling Holiday

By PAT CASTLE

These suggestions from the pen of one so famous and "dyed in the wool" in Scottish angling, should gladden the hearts of anglers who contemplate a Scottish fishing holiday. Mr. Castle's menu almost spoils the reader with choice. It is the offering of an experienced chef which cannot fail to please gourmet and gourmand alike.—ED.

IF you really want to hear and see Nature at its best, you should be on the banks of a stream at break of day on a bright morning in June. A mild sunrise usually means a good rise of trout on all rivers. No matter how badly fish may have been taking the previous day, or during the night, all the trout seem to move in search of food at break of day.

The rise may last only a few minutes, but on the other hand it may continue for an hour or two, until the sun is strong on the water. The commencement of the rise is the time to offer a cast of small spider flies, or better still, a small pink worm on 3 or 4x gut, casting upstream over the rising fish. I have found also that the minnow does well on all rivers during the grey of early morning, but when the sun strikes the water, it is practically useless.

Fishing a small worm up-stream is the finest art in angling, far ahead of either wet or dry fly fishing, and it takes a long time to learn—yes, it takes years to become expert. However, the art once mastered an angler can take good baskets under a clear bright sky and in low water—this when other lures are faring badly.

When worm fishing, disregard the still pools, but fish the shallow rapids, fish every little hide behind the stones.

A Scots Angling Holiday

From the River Dochart

Photo by friend of Author

It is better, you will find, to use no lead, allowing the worm to come down-stream without drag. It works far more naturally without lead. You will be surprised to find in how little water a good trout will lie at this season, sometimes their backs are hardly covered. Fish the most likely runs, covering all the water before you. If you kill a good trout at a certain stone or below a given bank, another such will be at that exact spot when you visit the stream again. You have discovered a good fishing lie.

Many years ago an ancient angler used to fish a well-known border river, starting in the morning and fishing up nearly three miles of water by evening. We nicknamed him the " Fleeing Fisher." He seldom spoke to other anglers, until one day I obliged him with two or three flies that were doing rather well. From then on he always had a passing word with me. I asked him one day why he covered so much water : " I have fished this water for over twenty years," he said, " and now try only those places where I have killed a good fish previously." He was fishing good feeding spots only !

Pat Castle

Invariably he was as successful as any of the " regulars " on this glorious stream, though far from being a good caster.

Border streams are particularly adapted to the method I have mentioned—the Kale, Bowmont, Etterick, Tarrow and the River Tweed. You may fish any of them for 2s. 6d. a day. The Whitadder for 2s. a day and the Haddingtonshire Tyne for only 1s. a day. On the other hand if you prefer really good loch fishing, go further north where, for the price of your hotel bill and the charge of a ghillie, you will get free fishing.

FOYERS, INVERNESS-SHIRE, is an excellent centre, set in a ring of good angling waters, Loch Garth and Faraline have lately been joined and now offer six miles of fine trouting. The fish average over half a pound and you will find an occasional two-pounder.

LOCH NESS provides salmon, sea trout and good brown trout. While the river Foyers itself is one of the beauty spots of the Highlands and swarms with small trout of an average weight of six ounces, some over three pounds in weight have been killed.

At GARVE, ROSS-SHIRE, on the river Black Water, there is three miles of free salmon fishing—plenty of fish run up the famous Falls of Rogie after the first flood in July. In addition sporting brown trout averaging about half a pound in weight may be caught in this lovely river.

LOCH LUICHART affords trout averaging three-quarters of a pound, but has yielded fish up to five pounds.

Again LOCH GARVE contains brown trout from half-pounders up to five pounds in weight.

At AULTNACEALGASH, ROSS-SHIRE, there are eight brown trout lochs and the fishing is excellent. Many specimens are to be seen in the hotel from three to ten pounds in weight—need one say more?

A Scots Angling Holiday

Photo by Author
Loch Awe

INCHNADAMPH, SUTHERLANDSHIRE, is practically on the banks of glorious LOCH ASSYNT, where salmon and good brown trout fishing is to be had.

LOCH AWE (not the loch in Argyll) is renowned for beautifully marked brown trout well over the half-pound average, while GILLAROO LOCH, about three miles distant, is believed to be the only loch in Scotland that holds the famous fighting Gillaroo trout ; they are here up to four pounds in weight.

The RIVER LOANAN, a quarter of a mile away, which runs between Loch Awe and Loch Assynt, affords good brown trout and salmon fishing from the end of July onwards.

ULLAPOOL has eight or nine lochs, the majority of which provide boats. Here the brown trout range from six ounces to two pounds in weight.

Pat Castle

Reflections in Loch Assynt   *Photo by Author*

ACHILTIBUIE, SUTHERLAND, can offer several good brown trout lochs, and really excellent sea trout fishing. The angler who penetrates this district " far from the madding crowd," will not be disappointed.

One word as to flies—imitate the natural whenever possible and don't fish larger than a number three in size. This size covers 95 per cent. of the naturals.

Try the blue Zulu dressed grey speckled instead of black hackle and you will be surprised.

Our next issue will be our Birthday Number. Order it now to make certain you get it. Our last issue was sold out within a month of publication! Don't be disappointed this time.—ED.

Printed in Great Britain
by Amazon